Also by Shulamit

<u>Beyond Words ~ The Sounds of the Kabballah</u>
Compact Disk
(ISBN # 1-929630-01-8)

BROOKLYN BODHISATTVAS

A Book of Visions
And Kabballistic Poetry

To JACK —
+ your magnificent
adventure

Shulamit

By Shulamit

For Chad and Deborah
Heart's Companions

Published in the United States by SoulSongs
Publications, a division of SoulSongs Inc., New York.
SoulSongs® is a registered Service Mark of
SoulSongs Inc.

SoulSongs Publications
SoulSongs Inc.
P.O.B. 465
High Falls, NY 12440

or

Poetry@SoulSongs.com

Library of Congress Cataloging-in-Publication Data

Brooklyn Bodhisattvas: A Book of Visions and
Kabballistic Poetry/by Shulamit/ –1ˢᵗ ED.

ISBN # 1-929630-02-6

Manufactured and printed at the
Sri Aurobindo Ashram Press, Pondicherry, India.
Published December 1999.

ACKNOWLEDGEMENTS

Many thanks to:
Deborah Barkow and Miranda Heathers for
their keen eye and heart wisdom;
My husband, Chad Elson, for his love and his
unwavering support;
Harold Akrongold for his appreciation and
encouragement;
My friends at Matagiri who helped in getting
this book printed: Julian & Wendy Lines,
Sam Spanier and Eric Hughes;
The Sri Aurobindo Ashram Press for clarity
and kindness across continents;
Karen Williams, for her patient assistance
and generous help with layout and design.

CONTENTS

BROOKLYN BODHISATTVAS

A TIGER IN THE GARDEN OF EDEN

MEMENTO MORI

THE DARK NIGHT OF THE SOUL

THE SOUND OF THE FLAME

THE BUTTERFLY EFFECT

BROOKLYN
BODHISATTVAS

BROOKLYN BODHISATTVAS

Brooklyn babes,
nubile, then pregnant,
dream of fine china,
a spandex-sleek ass,
and the high regard
of the highly regarded.

When the children,
grow to be the shadows
of the dream,
and what is lost is lost,
anxiety diminishes.

No time like the present.

Without gurus, mandalas
and celibacy
the Buddha belly laugh
arises out of unalloyed joy,
love suffuses and infuses,
and with easy grace,
cozy conversations
begin with the Angel of Death.

THE GARDEN OF EDEN

Adam after the Fall
was as terrified as you
before the Ascent.
The pleasures of the mind,
the longing of the flesh,
distracted him
from the terror of death.

Aching for what was lost -
telling himself
what he longed for
never was,
and never could be.

Across the frontier,
the Garden of Eden.
Sleeping on rocks
as soft as down.
Pineapples,
Sweetwater,
where none should be.

And you?
In bliss,
no desire, no fear,
no contrast
what kind of life is this?
Here Unity is not a flickering dream.
Life without struggle.
Life with no Death.

You have crossed this border before,
a prophet in Babylon,
with no audience excepting
an appreciative God.
Leaving the self-contained space
to go where you are Sent.

Into the Land of Lost Causes.

ROLLERBLADING HASIDS

Stuck in mud to the ankles,
forehead scanning the celestial -
The Messiah forever
taking His time -
a Hasid dreams
of rollerblading.

THE SOURCE

First the roar,
then the silence.
Either way -
Effort, no need.

Look up from rage
and terror;
Turn away
from the mirror.

There.

WISDOM

The earth
on which you stand
is detached
from its moorings.
Yet, it does not drift,
nor shift.

THE LAW OF MANIFESTATION

A canoe with no paddle
propelled by your wish,
a ladder produced
to scale a sheer cliff.
Effortless effort.
Climb aboard the Mother Ship.

SURRENDER

Say good bye to what was
and never could be
and rely on Me.

Water ski
without the rope.

IMAGE

Carried in a cherry picker
on a long vaulted pole
high above a stream bed
into the waterfall.

POWER

A King Cobra strikes
the back of the neck,
A meteor
burns cold.

The Unseen shimmers.

A TIGER IN THE
GARDEN OF EDEN

A TIGER IN THE GARDEN OF EDEN

Cries of yearning
reach the Garden gates
as sweet music.

A Tiger in the Garden of Eden
indolently observes
the naked Adam and Eve
without hunger.

Hearing the notes,
the Tiger
assumes his post
as border guard -
checking visas
for purity of intent.

Stalking the perimeter,
striking musculature
awaits the hopeful.
Observing a fierce demeanor,
and fearful of being consumed,
the formerly eager will not approach -
choosing suffering
over absorption.

CRAZY HORSE EXITS STAGE RIGHT

The soldier's musket trembles
beholding his captive's eyes.
The guard dissembles:
"Savage," he cries.

Crazy Horse calm
amidst the frenzy of treachery
and stolen victory,
observes conquerors
pumped up by booty,
acquisitiveness
proportionate to fear.

Grab land,
pave the Grand Tetons,
strip mine God's treasure,
leaving scarred sand.

Crazy Horse considers
his move.
The outcome is assured.
The soldier,
panicked by the size
of the captive's soul,
will bayonet -
obligingly opening
death's door.

And Crazy Horse
will ride again
in the world beyond the curtain.

THE SHAMAN

How do I get there from here?

A gourd filled with teeth,
tossed dice at a crap game:
a molar separates from the rest.

The molar splits,
Spitting mercury
and a map.
The mercury,
meaning obscure,
is seed to a vine.
The tendrils attach
to the ground, the chair,
to my hair.

I seize upon the map -
a linear answer:
To get from there to here,
memorize the lines.

The Shaman instructs:
"Do not study the map.
Swallow it."

It goes down
neat,
folded in eighths.
Undigested,
the wet paper
sticks.

And as divined so it is.

Opening out
at my translucent diaphragm,
the path unfolds
luminating a narrow gate.

THE TRANSFER

Beneath the Earth,
the Ant People
point the way
through tunneled paths,
into the Chamber.

The time has come
for the Transfer.
You always knew
the time would come.

Surrender keys,
picture ID's,
and the necessaries
for the Stranger's world.

The me that was,
is entombed.
The me that will be,
emerges -
strong ruthless, cold and clear,
all purpose and will,
without fear.

At the top of the canyon wall
broadcast the vibrational call.

The summoned -
restless listeners,
every cell alert for eons,
will assemble to
stretch across the crater
single file,

a band of radio waves
signaling position.

A VISIT WITH HERSELF

"How is your posture?"
She asked,
Present, but deeply occupied.

I slouch with awareness.

The Verdict: "Almost ready,"

"Now, Go."
She pronounced
"It is midnight."

THE ROPE

Place your ear.
Listen and attend
Earth's hidden beat.
Then heaven's note,
the Song of the Sacred Birds.
These two united
create the filament,
tensile and strong:

A rope to hold fast
in the coming inundation.

LA CASA DE LA LUNA

You can't go back
the way you came.
The road stopped,
a catastrophic drop.
Mirable dictu,
the car moved on.
Instead of hurling into abyss,
it hugged
a perpendicular path.
And you
tripped into this time.
Except it was a dream,
so it was myth
or was it?

La Casa de La Luna,
an idyllic spot
for sojourners,
Sea planes ferry the voyagers -
(Where?)

A clutched purse,
A young woman in an old woman's body,
Dreaming how far the others have gone.

The road may be visible
and longed for,
but impassable,
impossible.
You can't go back
the way you came.
No.

You must
go forward
to an unknown fate
without the landmarks
of self reflection.

Once you come
there will be few -

Bonhomie behind you.

TRIBAL MORES

Wandering
a lunar landscape
with no more singularity
than a rock,
I saw men
terrorized by the fade,
laboring together
in the sisyphean task
of making the
ephemeral last.

Touched by their grief,
their all consuming belief,
I joined in,
Re-turning to the dry well
to prime the pump.

Hypnotized -
the repetitive rhythm,
the perfume of co-mingled sweat -
I lingered anticipating
a savor,
a texture, a smell
the flavor
of an orgasmic Om.

PROPHECY

The day the Chamber door opens,
that day the world will stop.
We will draw back
the curtain of the universe
and slip in.

With your right hand,
protect
and with your left,
gather.

MAKING A GOLEM-A DREAM RECIPE

Lilliputs scale the body,
nesting comfortably,
indolently like spooning lovers,
in the folds and curves of the ears,
in the lid of the throat box,
and the ventricles
and auricles of the heart.

Their positions secured,
the Chief appends a translucent body
vessels visible,
he replaces the useless form -
and awaits the Breath
from which a Savior and Servant
will be born.

MILLENNIAL DREAMS

Wake up -
it could only be thus:
A comet hurled to earth,
the fiery dust
breeds a Phoenix
made of clay.

Desperately patient,
dreaming dangling morsels,
the few chew carrion.
Governments hide
in the underbelly,
quarry for Blackboots.

The touched but not touched,
steadfast in sorrow and joy,
wait for the turning.

THE MONK'S JOURNEY:
A VISION OF PAST,
PRESENT AND FUTURE

I.

Maintaining the moss garden,
listening to silence.
The rhythm of tasks
follow nature's calendar.
The gift of Time
and Sight.

Silence brings prophecy.
Folding the robes of isolation
the Monk voyages
in darkness
to warn the Heedless.

II.

At the camp,
the Chief of War,
(with mounting irritation:
Vegetarians!)
imprisons the Monk;
the prison no more confining
than a Monk's cell.

Slicing sounds, stilled struggle,
the odor of fear,
pierce protective bars,
in the night;

The prophecy fulfilled.

Confusing the incarcerated
Monk, with the enemy
of the enemy,
the Victor frees him,
smiling:
"Bear witness. All is lost."

God's janitorial crew assembles.
Jackal, Vulture, Crow
eat Ideologues and Lovers.

No difference in taste.

III.

To soothe his heart,
the Monk would tear
the Eyes from his head.
Having walked in the Way
and having changed
No Thing;
A witness to
blood impaled sadness,
madness;
spared to See.

Why men driven mad
with wanting
what cannot fulfill?

Why the beauty?
The moss garden?
The harmony?
Why sweet wisdom,
manna of the soul?
Why the kindness of the parents,
sacrificing all?
Contemplation
no greater value
than the ambition
of the Chief of War.

IV.

Hearing the cry,
A reply in vibration:
I give sweetness to you
Beloved Emanation,
for I know what is to come.

Witness to the Unbearable.
Faith in the Unknowable.

V.

And the Monk
arises from Despair
to journey,
sleeping against stone
through abandoned towns,
emptied by civil carnage
All that was known, gone.
Finding a clearing,
the Monk begins a fire
stoking the central flame
and carrying water
as before.

Survivors straggle
until nine gather.

VI.

Nearing the End,
the Monk asks
to see the moon rise.

The nine he cared for in life,
care for him in death
carrying him to the river deep.

The moon's reflection
Perfection.

He dies
gazing on the Sea
of Tranquillity,

Understanding
No Thing.

THE BARDO

Peering into time
at steamy sidewalks,
glistening sweat,
the hot fog
of a lover's breath.
A longing for more
than eternal life.

At the horizon,
walk the earth's
circumference.
Search for a way in.

Crossing the oceans of time
on the way to the vortex,
a temptation to form
brings grief and limitation.

At the inside of the earth,
beings who like it hot
stoke furnaces.

MEMENTO MORI

MEMENTO MORI

A prison without padlocks,
molasses replaces manacles.
Free association taboo.

When memory of original purpose
fades,
the Door is shown.

Recidivism is not unknown,
But it's rare.

The organism lurches toward freedom
and takes a shallow breath.

At the place where the breath sticks,
nostalgia makes its home.

THE PATH

Inflicted with partial blindness,
permitted to see through a haze.
Afflicted with sin to learn suffering,
Reality a pale reflection in Plato's cave.

Fear for the eyes confronting Vision:
Sight, like sunlight -
as panicked, unbandaged eyes Perceive.
The condemned man's reprieve.

Clarity like charity begins at Home.
A servant has no will of his own.

THE WITNESS

The figurehead
perfectly positioned
on the prow.

Consciousness,
but no free will.
Ideas,
but no hands.
Vigilance,
but no voice.
Bound by love
to protect.

Cascading hair,
Wings over the hull:
The angel,
in the front lines,
as the ship cuts the sea,
eye level shoals,
clear seas and
catastrophe.

Awareness fathoms,
sees and foresees;
but can prevent
No Thing.

ALIEN INVASION

Relax citizens,
they're not after you -
recalling to duty
emissaries from another time.

High technology enables tracking,
but mists and veils prevail.

Approaching Atmosphere,
blazes of sensation
obscure Reality.
Many mistake Otherness
for pathology.

Cries of confusion are heard.

The helping hand cannot always be touched.

THE ANGEL OF DEATH

When the Angel of Death
comes by, just repeat:
"I don't want to die."

Show your stuff,
add marketing fluff.
Think hair and life extensions,
plan to buy a new car.
Attend a positive thinking seminar.

THE HAPPINESS OF A STINGY MAN

A coin,
Clutched and clawed;
the savoring of dinner guests
who cancel.

THERAPY

Construct a monument
to the sharp stab
in the heart.
Bring constricted reality
to the air and light,
to Weather.

The chains incise
flesh of your leg.
Use that.
The animal gnaws its limb
for freedom.
Are you less?

The leg as *Monument*:
Bugs tidy the innards,
The flesh cures with time.

Then, a laminated placard;
cursive lettering,
chronological suffering,
line by line.

Grief resolved by
Graffiti.

CALCIFICATION

A calcified voice.
Breath wheezing
Over stripped muscle.
Even the capillaries
Atrophy below
The rusted defense line.

THE VICTIM

After a life
of cultivating bitterness,
the victim beholds
the dried peach pit of his life,
and notices with a start
the absence of fruit.

PERFECT POSTURE

What use is perfect posture
if life continues as before?

EVERYTHING MY MAMA
TAUGHT ME

Thoughtless,
I left open the door.
Now everything:
Heirlooms and Stratagems,
Gone.

LIES

Well, suppose it's all a lie,
celibates with girls on the side.
Defenders of the public good
snorting cash.
What does it get you
to know?
Without the lie,
Where?

The descended masters
despise us for our sins,
or better yet,
sin and exhort
faith for pain.

Looking at lies
outside,
inexorably leads
inside,
to Truth, and
terrifying change.

Living unforgivably:
transparent
with God's divinity.

Truthtellers
walk alone.
Consoled by the joy
of their soul song.

THE NIGHTMARE

Two men,
bulky, murderous
catch you unawares.

Moisten your mouth,
still your heart.
Pitch the tormentors
through the plate glass.

Even a child
can lift a dream.

FREEDOM

A gerbil on a wheel
does daily rotations,
mouthing and mounting,
repeating his mantra:

"I am a non-conformist,
I am a free man,
different from
the lockstep marchers."

CORPORATE BLISS

Captains of coaxial cables
and acetate overlays,
Segment the ventricles of the
human heart like markets:
and bowling alley hallwayed homes,
and syringes beyond shut doors
shall be yours.

THE PURSUIT OF HAPPINESS

Grasping, groping,
gasping, gaping.
Fleeing from pain
into the arms of hardship.
Put on a Disney face.
Nothing ever stays in place.

I lost a piece of myself early on.
Anyone seen it?

STRUGGLING

You are proud of your stroke,
and rightly so.
Practice has made it near perfect.
But why swim
on the hard wood
living room floor,
bemoaning wasted effort ?

RAGE

Is rage better than a ripe peach?
Once you eat the peach it's gone.

THE SEA WALL

Sometimes,
a wall of water
Stands.
Without any container.

It breaks according to its own inner rules.

THE DARK NIGHT
OF THE SOUL

THE DARK NIGHT OF THE SOUL

At the peak,
the vista is bleak:
Motorboats beached
where water once was,
A riverbed now a crater.

The crust cracking,
lava and larvae
erupting,
annihilating and creating,
without nostalgia.

Grace is not at issue.

Meanwhile,
no more lies.
Believe your eyes.

SIGNS OF SPRING

There's a hole in my will.
Vacated,
moved out.
And I,
motionless once again
await onrushing
direction.

Cheeky and saucy,
purpleyellow flowers
grow in gravel.

In this mood,
their insolence unravels.

THIRST

The stream is a puddle,
and the lake it fed is dry.

Now?

Drink despair.

ON THIN ICE

Ice skating at the center,
the perimeter begins to thaw.

A line of ice remains,
the thinness of a skating blade,
and you return to shore.

Men,
Controlled Impatience
await.
They'll even carry your skates.

MOSES AND AARON

So how do you think
it went for Moses?

Before meeting
the mighty Pharaoh,
Did he and Aaron laugh -
Remembering the time the sheep
stampeded
And the tent collapsed?

FOR SARTRE

The universe is silent.
The chatter of God's creatures
does not echo.

Cold air slices
the runner's lungs.
The predator's breath
crackles.

Consciousness
searching for meaning
turns in on itself.

THE SOUND OF
THE FLAME

THE SOUND OF THE FLAME

The Great Octave
plucked with the Breath of Life,
reverberates the spheres.
Vibrations -
the length
and breadth
of manifested creation.

Enveloping
the fruits,
Oscillations
return to the Source,
nurturing the Emanator.

The Flame listens and warms.

APOCALYPSE & EDEN

Apocalypse and Eden
Of what relevance?
The gate narrows.
Eclipsed Space.
Naked stare.
The mouth of eternity.

CREATION

A bulwark of fire,
The flames of Creation.

Hanging on the precipice of Eternity,
seemingly detached,
Man floats
as unaware as any fish
of the water in which it swims,
And on which it depends for life.

A DIFFERENT PERSON

You say you've Altered.
Your behavior and your insides.
I am not impressed.

Change is when you grow
Feathers -
wings sprout,
and architectural details
emerge from the back of your neck.

UNIVERSAL LAW

How to explain?
There is cause and effect,
and effort is rewarded by the by.
But when aligned with Universal Law
like Adam before the Fall,
all that is required
will materialize.

CONFUSED

The men throw
huge white jigsaw pieces
down the ravine,
and two keys
which tumble down after.
Until I yell up -
"Hey, we live down here!"

They disappear.
And with them the solution.

THE TURNING

Salt water freezes
A strange turning:
Sea creatures speechless

and men tug boats ashore
from dry land.

ETERNITY

Peeking through the keyhole,
Noticing belatedly there is no door.

Nothing hidden
or which separates
Except in the mind's eye.

UNISON

If you swim to the moon
On indigo not-wet water,
you will hear
Jeweled-Third-Eye birds,
White, with pulsating
robinegg blue tinted necks,
fly silently and in Unison.

THE BUTTERFLY
EFFECT

THE BUTTERFLY EFFECT

Observing a butterfly
in chrysalis state betrays nothing.
Only a blind man could detect
the Truth of its beauty at maturity.
Only a fool could believe
the gentle flutter of its wings
would effect the weather in Beijing.

Who would suspect thrones shake
from the power of the Fragile and the
Useless?

So it is at this moment -
A cocoon womb,
ripening pupa,
secreted from scathing disbelief
inside a protected cave.

If you wish to see,
slide the slippery slope
to the crater's center.
Through the hole
you can see them hanging.
More than one.

The New Race
looks like the old
but Knows.

ARACHNIDS

As guardians of the grid,
the consciousness of the spider
is wider than its web.

THE TIGER

The rope is frayed.
The tiger waits below.

We were as tight
as tigers and humans can be.
But you know cats.

It was never a pet.
Even now, it's not malevolent.
It's just doing its tiger thing.

Tigers can be great protectors
when they are in the mood.

Then again, people can make for great food.

XOCHIMILCO

The Dead walk.
Disappeared tribes,
their faces chalk,
hang in trees.

The air is full of regret:
difficult to forget,
even with materiality
no longer a reality.

When the primitives
were the sophisticates,
nature was god
and man a transitional creature
with no fixed address.

IN THE BELLY OF THE WHALE

Am I a volunteer?
Or was I press-ganged?

As the wise men say,
"There is free will,
but it is all ordained."

Possessed
of élan vital,
I had hoped
for the status quo.

Something
Easier on the vessel.

7

THE ELEPHANT

Riding on the broad neck
of a congenial elephant,
on the horizonless sea.

We do not speak
and have no bargain.

(a simple flick of his neck
and my lungs would explode)

Once ashore,
his trunk reaches back,
Purposefully,
gently
he sets me down.

ANTS

The Queen of the Ants,
Regal and Wise Wielding,
centrally controls the neurons
of Her workers,
as they route,
repair, refurbish
escape tunnels and supply lines.

Man, imprisoned in a linear mind,
thinks himself too big,

and anyway,
couldn't condescend to fit.

THE CHICKEN OR THE EGG

The effect:
At sweet sixteen,
my front teeth
developed their defect
and died.

The cause:
At fifty,
I had fallen like a tree limb
and landed on my chin.

About Shulamit

Shulamit is a spiritual teacher and one of the world's foremost sound-voice healers. Her work, using special sacred tones generated by the human voice, is the practical application of the wisdom and spiritual power of the ancient texts known as the Kabballah.

More information about Shulamit can be found on the web sites:

www.SoulSongs.com
and
www. Kabballah.com

or by writing to:

SoulSongs®
P.O.B. 465
High Falls, NY
USA 12440